PRINTED IN U.S.A.

BATS

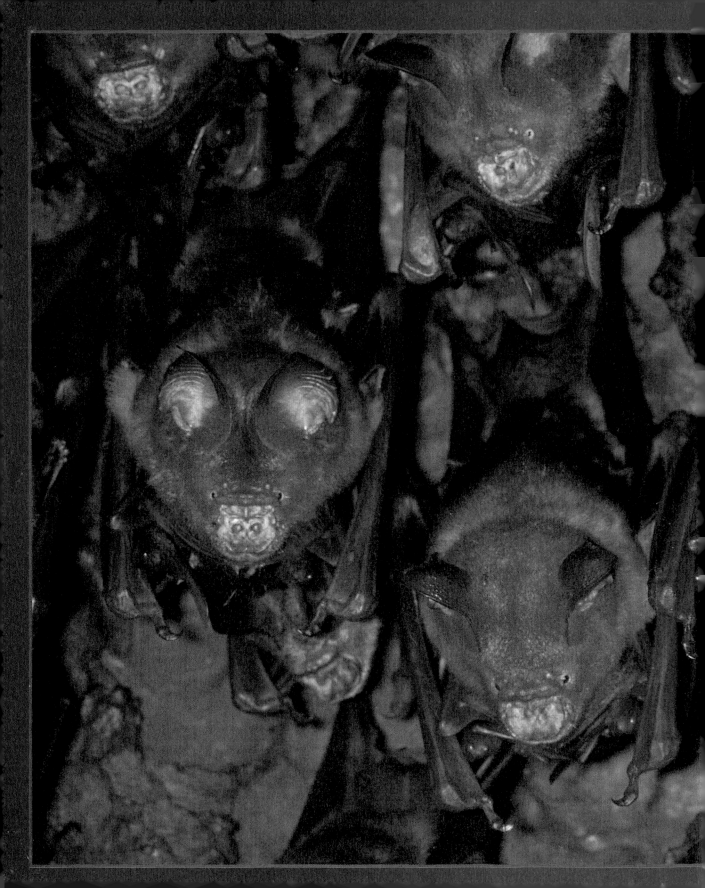

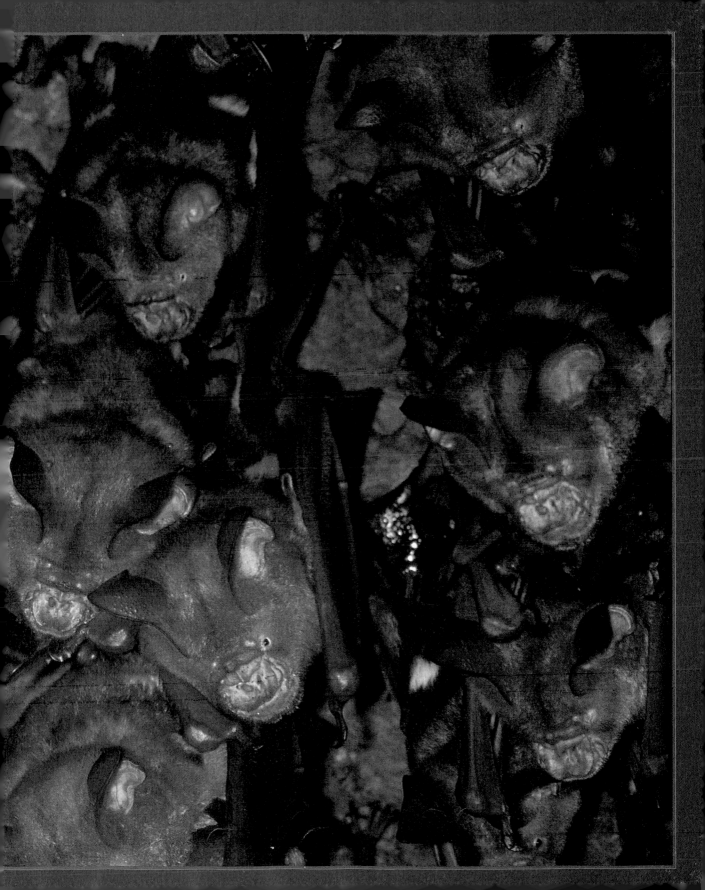

Photo credits:

Russell C. Hansen: page 12
Michael P. Turco: pages 24-25
Norbert Wu: pages 13, 28
Merlin Tuttle/Bat Conservation International: cover; page 6, 8, 10, 13, 16, 19, 24, 26, 28
Hans Christoph Kappel/BBC Natural History Unit: page 7
Dietmar Nill/BBC Natural History Unit: page 6
Stanley Breeden/DRK: pages 14-15, 20, 21, 29
John Cancalosi/DRK: pages 6, 18-19
Michael Fogden/DRK: cover; pages 7, 8, 16-17
Stephen J. Krasemann/DRK: pages 10, 11, 22-23
Wayne Lankinen/DRK: page 6
Sid & Shirley Rucker/DRK: page 22
Belinda Wright/DRK: pages 15, 28-29
L. Hugh Newman/NHPA: page 15
NHPA: page 27
Anthony Mercieca/Photo Researchers: page 28
Stephen Dalton/Photo Researchers: pages 10, 12, 13,
David Hosking/Photo Researchers: cover
Jeff Lepore/Photo Researchers: page 23
Rexford Lord/Photo Researchers: pages 9, 17
Karen Marks/Photo Researchers: page 25
William E. Townsend Jr./Photo Researchers: page 17
Merlin Tuttle/Photo Researchers: page 7, 9, 11, 14, 18, 19, 20, 2125, 26
Jonathan Watts/ Photo Researchers: page 15
Walt Anderson/Visuals Unlimited: pages 20-21
Bill Beatty/Visuals Unlimited: page 27
Thomas Gula/Visuals Unlimited: page 17
Joe McDonald/Visuals Unlimited: page 8
William Palmer/Visuals Unlimited: page 23
Nada Pecnik/Visuals Unlimited: page 29
Rick & Nora Bowers/Wildlife Collection: pages 11, 19, 29
Martin Harvey/Wildlife Collection: page 22
A. Maywald/Wildlife Collection: page 24

Scientific Consultant:
Barbara French
Conservation Information Specialist
Bat Conservation International

For even more information on bats, contact
Bat Conservation International (BCI) at P.O.
Box 162603, Austin, Texas, 78716-2603.
Their web site is at http://www.batcon.org

Copyright © 1997
Kidsbooks, Inc.
3535 West Peterson Ave.
Chicago, IL 60659

Manufactured in the United States of America

EYES ON NATURE ™

BATS

**Written by
Celia Bland**

kidsbooks®
Incorporated

GOING BATTY

Tonight, step outside into the darkness. Do you hear the flap, flap of unseen wings? Are small shapes flitting among the trees? You have caught a glimpse of the most fantastic night-fliers of the natural world—bats.

IS IT A BIRD

Ancient people though bats were featherles birds. We know nov that bats, like humans, are mammals. The are warm-blooded and they nurse their babies. But, unlike humans bats can fly!

▲ Other mammals that come close to flying, such as flying squirrels, use the winglike flaps of skin between their arms and legs to glide.

▲ The spotted bat has a black-and-white coat, pink wings, and enormous pink ears.

FUR FASHIONS

Mammals have fur, and bats are no exception. Those that roost outside have longer hair than those that roost in caves. Like cats, bats clean their fur using their tongue and claws. Although many bats are brown or gray, others are yellow, orange, white, or red. Some are so brightly colored, they're known as butterfly bats.

These Honduran white ▶ bats have snow-white fur.

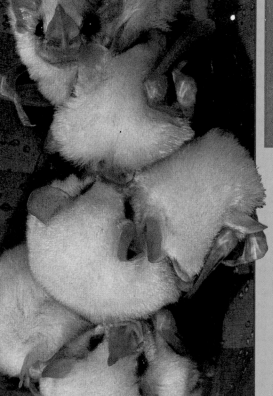

DINOSAUR TIMES ▲

Fossil evidence shows that bats have been around for at least 50 million years. Some scientists think bats have been around even longer. Bats may have swooped around the huge heads of the dinosaurs 60 million years ago!

6

The smallest bat in North America, the pipistrelle, measures two and a half inches and fits neatly into a walnut shell!

ALL SIZED UP

The smallest bat is the smallest of all mammals— Thailand's Bumblebee bat, which weighs less than a penny. The largest bats are the flying foxes of Asia, some of which have a wingspan of six feet—about the length of a surfboard! Their body is about one and a half feet long.

BLIND AS A BAT

Many people think that bats are blind. In fact, some bats see well in dim light. Other bats see less well. But all bats have other, strong senses that help them find food in the dark, and help them navigate when flying.

Vampire bats have razor-sharp teeth for slicing through skin!

DENTAL PLANS

A bat's teeth and the shape of its mouth are adapted to the type of food it eats. Fruit bats have large flat teeth for grinding pulpy fruit. Insect-eaters have jagged teeth in their cheeks that can slice and grind an insect's hard outsides.

BIG DIET

You may think of bats as blood-suckers. But in the real bat world, a bat diet may include fruit, leaves, pollen, cacti, insects, frogs, fish, spiders, lizards, and other bats! Bats are actually categorized into two groups—the large fruit-eating megabats, and the smaller microbats, most of which eat insects.

▲ The long-nosed bat licks the fruit of an organ-pipe cactus.

7

LOTS OF LOOKS

You can find bats throughout most of the world, in forests, deserts, jungles, and in your own backyard! There are close to 1,000 different species. With so many different varieties, it only seems logical that some bats would look a little more unusual than others.

▲ STRANGE MATES

Little brown bats may be the most common bats in the U.S. and Canada. Covered with thick brown fur, the little brown bat weighs only one-quarter ounce! It often shares its roost with the big brown bat, near a river, marsh, or lake. There it catches as many as 1,200 "night-flying" insects in one night!

GOTHIC GARGOYLES

The gothic bat gets right to the point! At the tip of its nose is a long sword, almost as long as the bat's ears. These bats are found in tunnels and other structures in South and Central America.

WHAT A HAIRDO!

The award for best bat hairdo most certainly goes to Chapin's free-tailed bat. This African dweller sports a two-colored crest on top of its head. Like male bats of many species, a male Chapin's bat has scent glands that are used to attract females. The crest helps spread the male's perfume.

TRUE OR FALSE? ▶
People used to believe that the false vampire bat of Latin America drinks the blood of animals just like true vampire bats do. Actually, this bat eats small animals, such as lizards and birds, as well as fruit.

THAT'S A BAT? ▼
Not all bats are scary-looking. Some megabats are called flying foxes because they have narrow foxlike snouts, pointed ears, and a furry brown coat.

SCARY FACES ▲
Does the thought of a bat make you cringe? There are some strange-looking bats flying around out there. The horseshoe bat, named for the outline of its U-shaped nose, is one of Europe's most common bats. It is so small, it can fit inside a match box.

▼ The lobed-forehead bat from South America has a spooky-looking face!

9

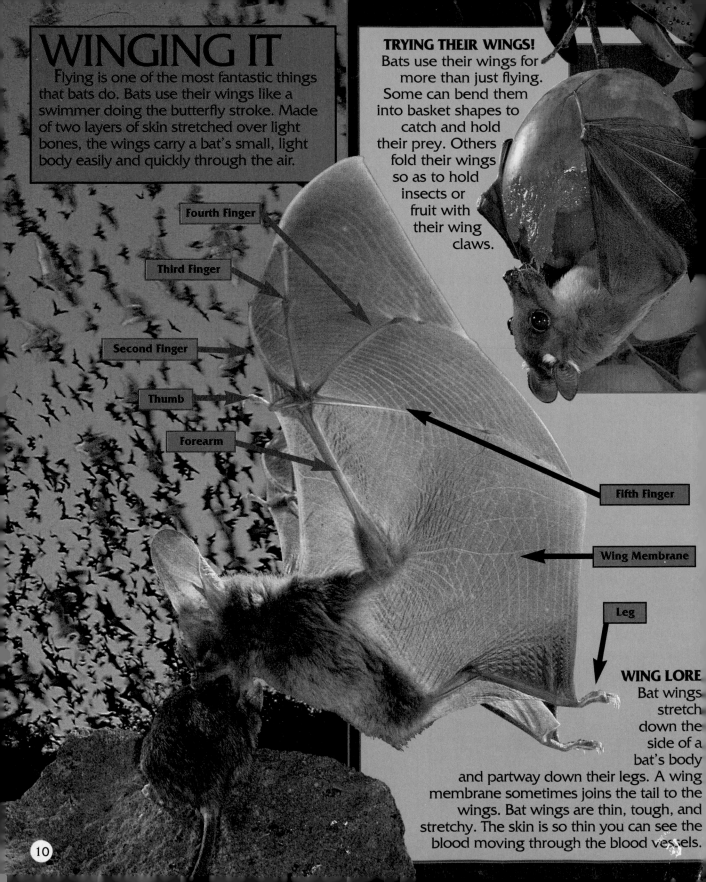

WINGING IT

Flying is one of the most fantastic things that bats do. Bats use their wings like a swimmer doing the butterfly stroke. Made of two layers of skin stretched over light bones, the wings carry a bat's small, light body easily and quickly through the air.

TRYING THEIR WINGS!

Bats use their wings for more than just flying. Some can bend them into basket shapes to catch and hold their prey. Others fold their wings so as to hold insects or fruit with their wing claws.

Fourth Finger

Third Finger

Second Finger

Thumb

Forearm

Fifth Finger

Wing Membrane

Leg

WING LORE

Bat wings stretch down the side of a bat's body and partway down their legs. A wing membrane sometimes joins the tail to the wings. Bat wings are thin, tough, and stretchy. The skin is so thin you can see the blood moving through the blood vessels.

KNEE ▶ ACTION

It's a good thing that bats can fly so well. They have legs, but are not very skillful at walking. A bat's knees bend backward, which makes these creatures very clumsy on the ground.

HANGING OUT

On their wings, bats have a thumb and four long jointed fingers that are enormous compared to the size of their body. If you were a bat, your fingers would be longer than your legs! Bats also have hooked claws on their wings and toes which help them hang by their feet and climb along a wall or tree trunk. To leave their roosts, they simply fall towards the ground, flapping their wings until they take flight.

BIG GULP

Bats like to drink "on the wing." They fly over streams or ponds, slurping up water from midair. If they fly too low they go swimming, using their wings as paddles to push themselves through the water.

The long tail of a ▶ free-tailed bat may help It navigate.

SUPER FLIERS

Mexican free-tailed bats are just one of 80 kinds of free-tailed microbats. They can fly 10,000 feet above the ground and, catching tailwinds, reach speeds of 60 mph— that's as fast as a car and as high-flying as an airplane!

WING SHAPES

Big brown bats have short broad wings for quick changes of direction. Mexican free-tails have longer narrower wings, perfect for long-distance flying. The Honduran white bat's short stubby wings let it hover in place like a helicopter.

THE LITTLE ONES

Megabats may be bigger in size, but microbats rule when it comes to numbers. There are 750 species of microbats. They are found on every continent except Antarctica, and in every landscape except the hottest deserts and the coldest polar regions.

BAT MACHINE

Bat scientists use a device called a bat detector to change high-pitched bat calls to sounds people can hear. This machine can help locate and sometimes even identify bats in caves or other dark habitats.

EAR-SIGHT

Microbats have a particular talent for "seeing" with their ears, called *echolocation*. They fly with their mouth open, sending out high-pitched noises—called *ultrasounds*—which bounce off objects. The "echo" returns to the bat. If the echo returns quickly, the bat knows that an insect, rock, or tree is nearby.

LISTEN UP

Talk about good hearing! California leaf-nosed bats, which live in the lowland desert areas of the western U.S. and Mexico, can find bugs by listening for their footsteps or wing beats. They can even hear a cricket hopping!

Unlike many other microbats, the horseshoe bat sends ultrasounds through its nose.

NOSE LEAVES

Some bats have folds of skin around their nostrils. These are called nose leaves. Scientists believe that nose leaves help with the process of echolocation by aiming a bat's sound waves in different directions.

Frog-eating bat ▶

◀ FALSE VAMPIRE

The false vampire bat is the world's biggest microbat, measuring three feet from wing tip to wing tip.

▶ BIG EARS

The false vampire bat's huge ears are better to hear with. Big ears aid hearing by trapping more sounds. Many bats can tell the direction and speed of flying insects just by listening! This helps them find food in total darkness.

BIG BATS

Megabats "hang out" in warm areas, particularly near the equator. One hundred and fifty species live in Africa, India, Southeast Asia, the East Indies, and Australia. They eat fruit and flower nectar, which is plentiful year-round in tropical climates.

MEGA-SENSE

Unlike microbats, most mega-bats cannot echolocate. Notice how small their ears are! Megabats depend on other senses. Their large eyes, which can see very well, and their powerful sense of smell help them find ripe fruit at night.

▲ BABY ON BOARD

The Gambian epauletted bat is very "attached" to its offspring. This mother takes her pup with her when she goes searching for food. The baby hangs on to her belly fur with its strong claws as she flies, and shares the sweet fruit she finds.

◀ NECTAR NOSE

The nostrils of tube-nosed megabats open at the ends of short tubes. The bats stick these tube-like snouts deep into sweet-smelling flowers and suck up a tasty meal of nectar.

MEGA CLAWS

Megabats have an extra feature which helps them to hold fruit with their wings— a claw on their second finger. These claws are an easy way for amateur bat-watchers to identify fruit bats.

COOLING OFF

When flying foxes roost in the branches of large trees, they wrap their huge wings around their upside-down body to keep warm. On hot days, they cool off by fanning their wings.

SPECTACLES

The spectacled flying fox gets Its name from the light rings around its eyes. Like other flying foxes, this bat lives where it is warm all year long. A powerful flier, it might travel as far as 20 miles to reach a favorite fruit orchard.

A DRINK OF BLOOD

No bat has been so feared and misunderstood as the vampire bat—the only bat that feeds on blood. Just forget those Count Dracula movies! Vampires rarely bite people or kill their prey. And an animal bitten by a vampire bat will not bleed to death, though it may contract a disease.

WHO'S WHO?

Vampire bats live in Mexico, Central America, and South America. The common vampire bat preys on cattle, horses, and other livestock. The hairy-legged vampire (above) targets birds. White-winged vampires feast on both mammals and birds.

WILD WALKER

All bats are great fliers, but the vampire bat is a great walker. The vampire can jump on all four legs like a frog, leap straight up into the air, or walk around on two legs like a monkey! This one is doing a handstand.

DEAD OF NIGHT

Most active on dark nights, a vampire can circle its prey unseen and land lightly on its head or back. Hopping gently on the thumbs and soles of its feet, it doesn't even waken the sleeping cow or chicken— even when it takes a bite!

NO SUCKER!

A common vampire doesn't suck blood. It laps it up. The bat has heat-sensitive pits on its face that help it pick a choice spot to bite. Then, using its razor-sharp teeth to cut a shallow wound in its prey, it presses its lower lip against the wound and starts licking!

JUST A DROP

The common vampire drinks about one ounce of blood a night. Blood is very thick. If a vampire drank too much, it would become too heavy to fly away!

By helping each other, vampire ▲ roost-mates help their species to survive.

HELPING OUT

Vampire bats are known to care for orphaned pups. They also feed other adults, which can be a life-saving act. If a vampire bat goes hungry for two days, it will die.

NIGHT HUNTERS

Meat-eating bats have good reasons for their nocturnal schedules. When they fly out at night to hunt for insects, fish, or small animals, most of their competition is sleeping.

A little big-eared bat holds its katydid prey. ▶

TEETH TALE

When the oldest bat fossil was found in North America, scientists were amazed by how little bats have changed over the last 50 million years. The fossil's teeth showed that this prehistoric bat, like most of today's bats, was an insect-eater.

SCOOPING INSECTS

Most bats eat insects, catching their prey in their mouth or using their wings or tail membranes to scoop the insects up. Small insects are eaten "on the wing." Larger ones may be eaten while the bat hangs from its roost by one foot and uses the other to hold its meal up to its mouth.

◀ FROG-EATERS

Frog calls are inaudible to us, but not to the frog-eating bats of Mexico and southern Brazil. Not only can they follow a frog's call and catch a juicy morsel, but they can distinguish who's bite-sized and who's poisonous.

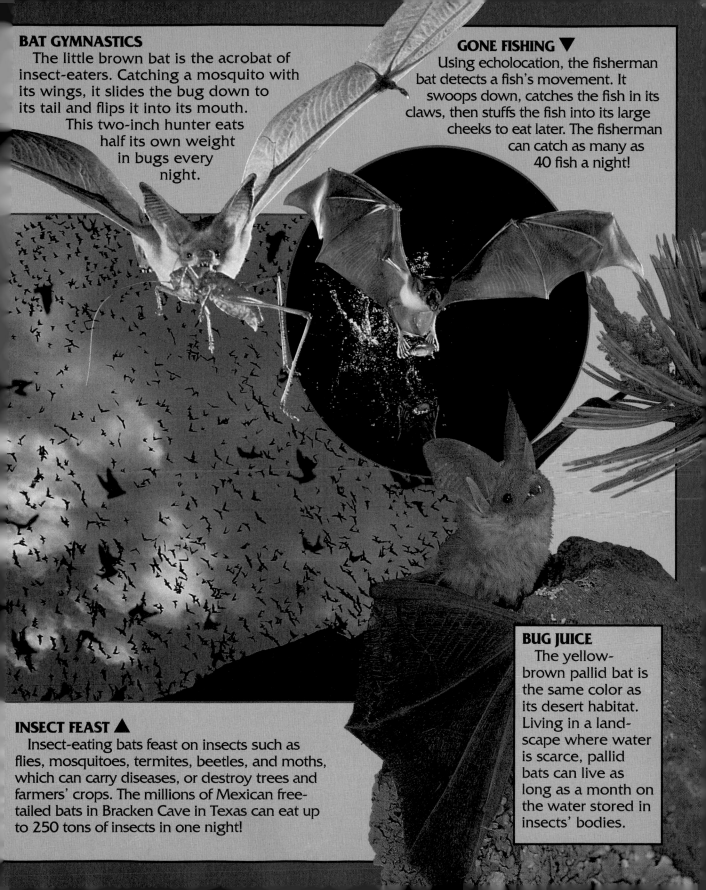

BAT GYMNASTICS

The little brown bat is the acrobat of insect-eaters. Catching a mosquito with its wings, it slides the bug down to its tail and flips it into its mouth. This two-inch hunter eats half its own weight in bugs every night.

GONE FISHING ▼

Using echolocation, the fisherman bat detects a fish's movement. It swoops down, catches the fish in its claws, then stuffs the fish into its large cheeks to eat later. The fisherman can catch as many as 40 fish a night!

INSECT FEAST ▲

Insect-eating bats feast on insects such as flies, mosquitoes, termites, beetles, and moths, which can carry diseases, or destroy trees and farmers' crops. The millions of Mexican free-tailed bats in Bracken Cave in Texas can eat up to 250 tons of insects in one night!

BUG JUICE

The yellow-brown pallid bat is the same color as its desert habitat. Living in a land-scape where water is scarce, pallid bats can live as long as a month on the water stored in insects' bodies.

This Gambian fruit bat is feasting on figs.

FRUIT BATS

Although some bats eat a combination of fruit and insects, others eat fruit or nectar almost exclusively. Flying foxes chew and suck on fruit, swallowing the juice and spitting out the pulp.

Baobab tree

◀ **LEAF TREATS**
Although they get most of their nutrients from fruits, some fruit-eaters have to eat a certain amount of insects for protein. Fruit-eaters can also get protein from leaves. They soften the leaves in their mouth, swallow the liquid, and spit out the rest.

Bats help pollinate cacti and other flowering plants.

GIVING LIFE

Known as the "Tree of Life" because of its importance to other wildlife in Africa, the baobab (BAY-uh-bab) tree depends on bats to help it pollinate. Baobab flowers bloom at night, attracting nectar-eating bats. Pollen comes off on these bats' fur as they feed, and when they fly from blossom to blossom they carry the pollen with them!

Dipping its long tongue into a banana flower, this fruit bat finds a tasty meal.

◀ SMALL BUT FIERCE

The Queensland blossom bat has bristles on the tip of its tongue to help it lap up nectar. Don't be taken in by its delicate looks. It will attack any bat that elbows in on its territory!

BAT HEROES

Bananas, papayas, mangoes, avocados, and desert plants such as organ-pipe cacti rely on bats for pollination. Bats are responsible for scattering up to 95% of the seeds needed for new trees in the tropical rain forests.

21

TO THE BAT CAVE!

The place where a bat sleeps is called a *roost*. Some roosts are beds for only one or two bats. Other roosts are huge cities of thousands or even millions of bats. One popular roosting place is in caves.

WHERE TO GO?

Like most animals, bats have to adapt to colder temperatures and limited food during winter. Some migrate south to warmer climates where food is more plentiful. Others hibernate until spring. The European barbastelle does both, going south to hibernate in caves!

TURNING HEADS

Along the walls of a cave, a bat can grasp any little nook with its claws, and hang upside down. While roosting, it can turn its head right-side up and look around. A bat's neck is so flexible, it can even turn its head backwards!

STAYING COOL

During hibernation, bats live on fat they stored during the summer. Their breathing slows down and their heart rate may drop from 400 to 25 beats a minute. They may sleep for as long as five months without eating or drinking.

FISHERMAN'S FRIEND

The silver-haired bat roosts alone and migrates alone, flying thousands of miles to warmer climates. It has even been found on ships' masts out at sea, probably having been blown off course by a storm.

WHAT A CROWD!

Very sociable, Mexican free-tailed bats summer in U.S. caves. More than 20 million congregate in Texas's Bracken Cave, and 50,000 live in New Mexico's Carlsbad Caverns. When winter comes, they migrate south—1,500 miles to central Mexico.

WATER WEAR

As a bat hibernates, water from the cold air settles on its warm body. This condensation is a perfect refreshment when the bat wakes up thirsty!

EXCEPTIONAL ROOSTS

Caves are not the only roosting spots for bats. Bats hang out in trees, mines, tunnels, old buildings, bridges, bushes, abandoned termite nests, and tropical spider webs—anywhere they can sleep in safety and seclusion.

▼ An attic is a great place for bats to hang out.

The rafters in a barn are a welcome home to weary bats.

LEAF ARCHITECTS

Tiny tent-building bats roost in palm leaves in the jungles of Central and South America. To make a leaf "tent" to protect them from the rain, sun, and wind, these bats chew holes in the central rib of a big palm leaf until the leaf folds in half. The holes are then used as claw holds.

24

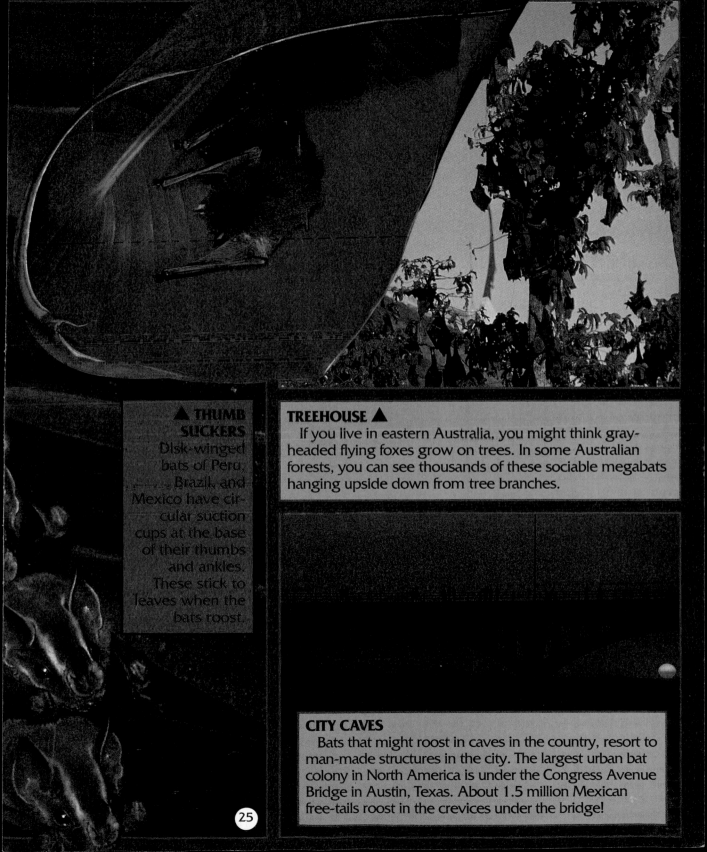

▲ THUMB SUCKERS
Disk-winged bats of Peru, Brazil, and Mexico have circular suction cups at the base of their thumbs and ankles. These stick to leaves when the bats roost.

TREEHOUSE ▲
If you live in eastern Australia, you might think gray-headed flying foxes grow on trees. In some Australian forests, you can see thousands of these sociable megabats hanging upside down from tree branches.

CITY CAVES
Bats that might roost in caves in the country, resort to man-made structures in the city. The largest urban bat colony in North America is under the Congress Avenue Bridge in Austin, Texas. About 1.5 million Mexican free-tails roost in the crevices under the bridge!

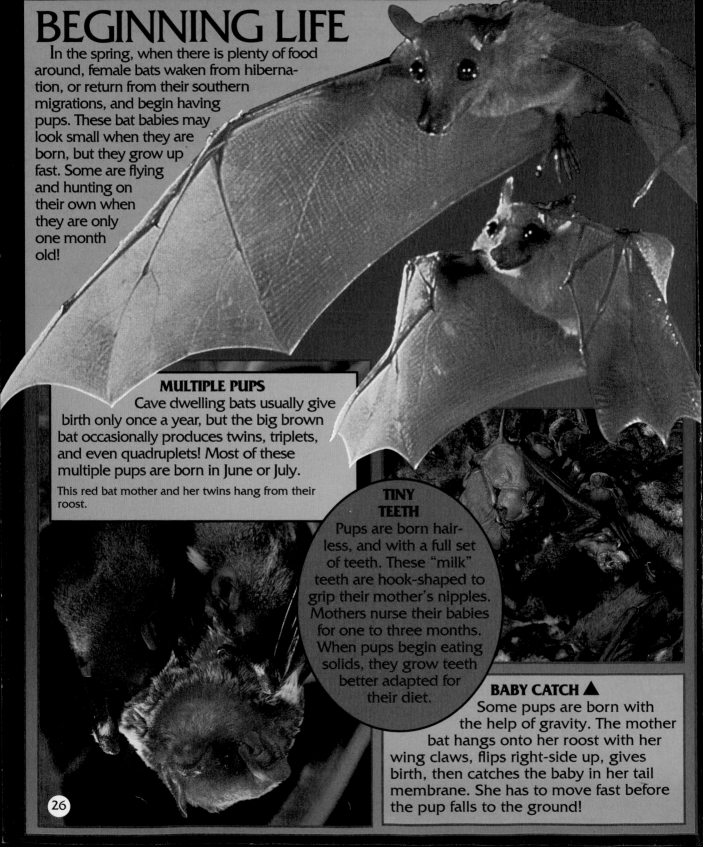

BEGINNING LIFE

In the spring, when there is plenty of food around, female bats waken from hibernation, or return from their southern migrations, and begin having pups. These bat babies may look small when they are born, but they grow up fast. Some are flying and hunting on their own when they are only one month old!

MULTIPLE PUPS

Cave dwelling bats usually give birth only once a year, but the big brown bat occasionally produces twins, triplets, and even quadruplets! Most of these multiple pups are born in June or July.

This red bat mother and her twins hang from their roost.

TINY TEETH

Pups are born hairless, and with a full set of teeth. These "milk" teeth are hook-shaped to grip their mother's nipples. Mothers nurse their babies for one to three months. When pups begin eating solids, they grow teeth better adapted for their diet.

BABY CATCH ▲

Some pups are born with the help of gravity. The mother bat hangs onto her roost with her wing claws, flips right-side up, gives birth, then catches the baby in her tail membrane. She has to move fast before the pup falls to the ground!

HANGERS ON
Newborn pups are already experts at hanging around! As soon as they are born, they cling to their mother as she roosts, or to the roost itself. Because hanging on is so important, pups are born with strong feet and legs, and sharp claws. If a baby bat loses its grip and falls to the ground, it will most likely die.

SPECIAL VOICE
When a female bat returns to the nursery after hunting, how can she tell which of the many pups is hers? Easy! She recognizes its voice! And just to make sure she has found the right one, she smells and licks it. Only after it has passed these tests does she allow the hungry little bat to begin nursing.

ONE AND ONLY
Many small mammals have litters of seven or more babies once or twice a year. Almost all female bats give birth to only one baby once a year. This means that it can take a long time for bat colonies to recover if a roost is disturbed and bats are killed.

NURSERY CAVES
Some caves house millions of bats. In the Mexican free-tail nurseries in Bracken Cave, there can be as many as 500 babies per square foot! Bats often return to the same nursery site year after year. Scientists believe that the bat nursery at Carlsbad Caverns has been in use for 17,000 years!

▶ These bats have been tagged and accounted for!

BAT ALERT

Over half of the bats in the U.S. and Canada are threatened or endangered. Scientists keep a close eye on endangered bats. They tag them, trace migrations, and monitor populations.

IN CAVES

If you visit a bat cave during the winter, don't disturb the bats! They can use an entire month's supply of fat trying to escape, and may starve before spring. Vandals at the Eagle Creek Cave in Arizona, once the world's largest colony, have reduced 30 million bats to 30,000!

UGLY RUMORS

Bats aren't dangerous to people. They do not get tangled in people's hair, and they do not "carry" rabies. Bats *can* "contract" rabies like any other wild animal can. For this reason, you should never handle them.

▼ It takes patient observation to study bats.

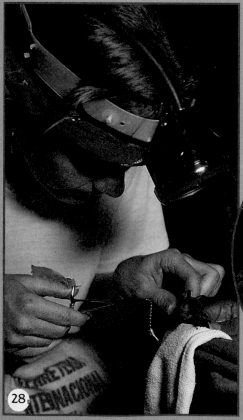

◀ Tagging a tiny bat requires a delicate and careful hand.

NATURAL FOES ▲

A number of animals prey on bats. Snakes climb to roosting places. Opossums, raccoons, and skunks prey on bats that fall to the ground. Owls and hawks catch bats as they emerge at dusk to hunt.

BAT HOUSE ▼

Because bats are losing a lot of their traditional roosting areas, people are building bat houses to make up for this loss. As many as 200 bats can fit in a house just two feet high. When mosquitoes began overwhelming the Florida Keys, a huge house was built to attract these masters of pest control.

◄ SPECIAL TREATMENT

Don't touch a hair on the head of Hawaii's only bat. Named for the silvery tips on their fur, hoary bats are so rare on the island, people can be jailed for disturbing them.

► IT'S THE LAW!

Because flying foxes eat fruit crops, many are being hunted and killed. People either don't know, or forget, that fruit bats actually help fruit to grow by spreading seeds around. Without bats to spread seeds and pollen, many tropical and subtropical forests around the world could not survive. Flying foxes are now protected by law in Australia's Ku-ring-gai preserve.

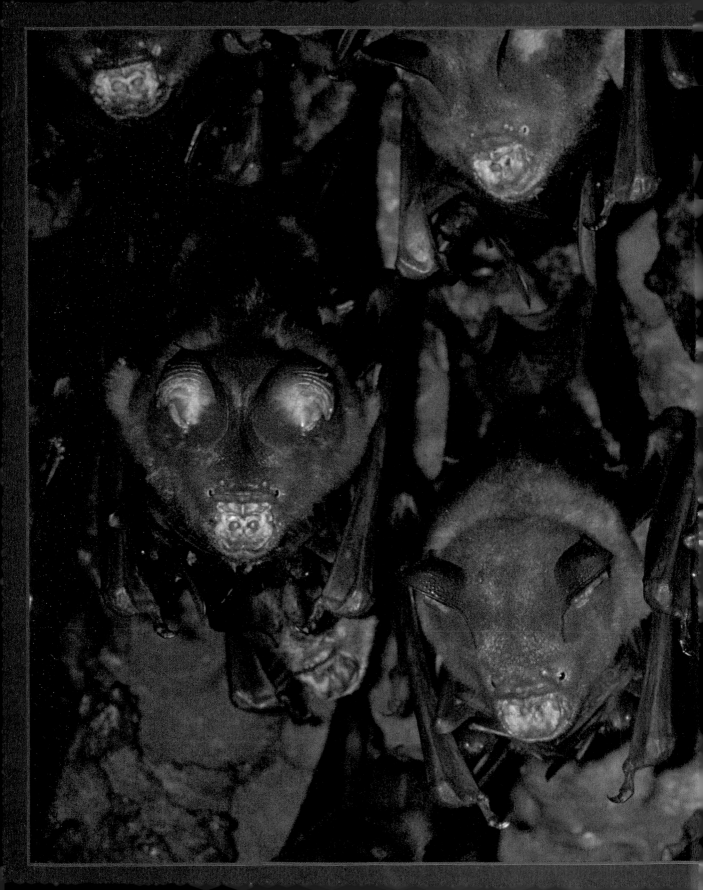

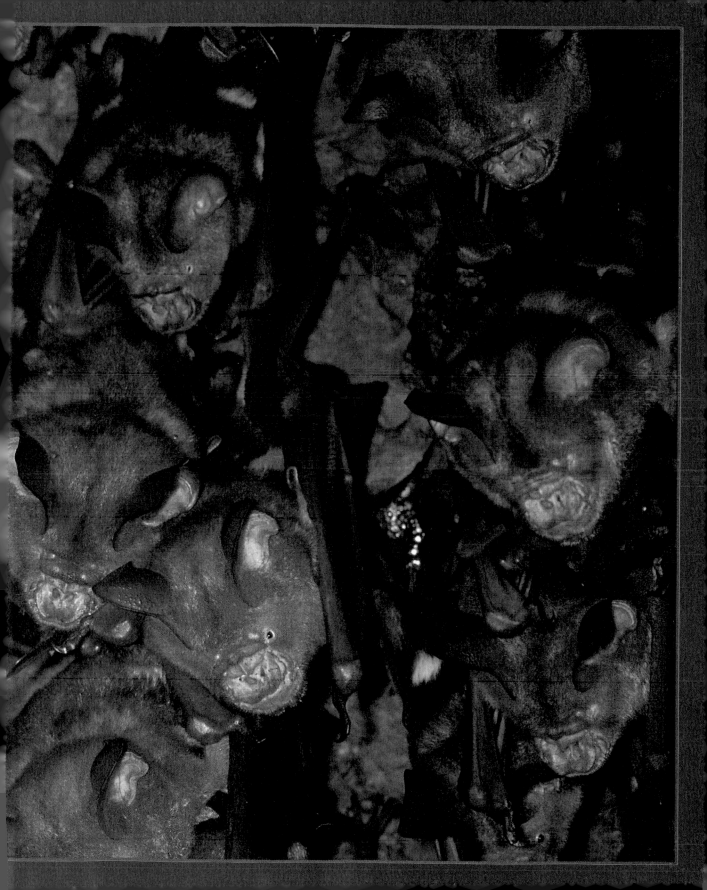